AFTER 40: MEANING OF LIFE JOURNAL

AFTER 40
MEANING OF
LIFE
JOURNAL

Prompts and Practices for
Self-Discovery and Finding Purpose

JULIE A. LEVIN, MA, MFT

R

ROCKRIDGE
PRESS

For general information on our other products and services or to obtain technical support, please contact our Customer Care Department within the United States at (866) 744-2665, or outside the United States at (510) 253-0500.

Rockridge Press publishes its books in a variety of electronic and print formats. Some content that appears in print may not be available in electronic books, and vice versa.

TRADEMARKS: Rockridge Press and the Rockridge Press logo are trademarks or registered trademarks of Callisto Media Inc. and/or its affiliates, in the United States and other countries, and may not be used without written permission. All other trademarks are the property of their respective owners. Rockridge Press is not associated with any product or vendor mentioned in this book.

Interior and Cover Designer: Sean Doyle
Art Producer: Sara Feinstein
Editor: Mo Mozuch
Production Manager: David Zapanta
Production Editor: Melissa Edeburn

Illustration used under license from Creative Market. Author photo courtesy of Jason Elhaderi.

Paperback ISBN: 978-1-63878-672-6
R0

THIS JOURNAL BELONGS TO:

_____

CONTENTS

INTRODUCTION

Journaling has long been a powerful tool for self-exploration and growth because writing can help you make connections and discoveries that thinking alone can't. Through journaling you might discover a passion from which you turned away or you might let go of obligations that have never served you. You might discover that your wisdom and insights make you an important member of a group. You might find deep satisfaction in solitary hours spent following your curiosity wherever it leads.

The beauty of midlife is that you don't have to follow a script. No one else knows what's right for you. The answers are within. This journal will help you clarify your feelings, wishes, and needs. Its questions and prompts are designed to help you create a life that you love—to find the time, energy, and environment you need to thrive.

Journaling in my forties and fifties has helped me make significant, positive changes in my career, my relationships with others, and, most important, my relationship with myself. I've created a life that feels perfectly suited to my values, my tastes, even my circadian rhythm. I've learned to listen deeply to my feelings and needs. Fulfilling those needs instead of ignoring them, as "just do it" culture instills, has led me to more self-trust and self-love.

It is a joy to share these processes with you so you can find meaning and fulfillment in the next stage of your life. I joke that we are at the intersection of gravitas and gravity—our gray hair and wrinkles are hard won. We have paid our dues. Now it is time to reap the rewards. The goal is to discover what those rewards will be for you.

HOW TO USE THIS BOOK

You are the boss of this book. Some of the exercises build on previous chapters and prompts. But if something later in the book calls to you, feel free to go there. If you come to an exercise that draws on earlier work, you can always go back to it. Trust your curiosity.

A regular writing practice, like meditation, can enhance creativity and critical thinking. Commit to 5 or 10 minutes every day so writing doesn't feel like a chore. Some days you may want to write more. That's fine, too.

Make journaling sacred. Find a time and space where you won't be distracted. Pour your favorite beverage. Set an intention for kindness and curiosity. Light a candle or put out a photo of someone who believes in you. You are envisioning a future that brings you satisfaction. Taking time to listen to your hopes and wishes signals that you care about yourself. Imagine sending gratitude to your caring self, and do your best to savor every moment you give yourself the time and attention you need to thrive.

NOTE: These exercises should leave you feeling excited, motivated, and grounded in self-awareness. If you find yourself struggling with anxiety, depression, or painful self-criticism, please seek out a trained therapist for support and guidance. The Resources section at the end of the book includes directories where you can find licensed therapists.

PART 1

Get to Know Yourself (Again)

When my friend Libbie and I visited the La Brea Tar Pits, she suddenly stopped midstride and said, "I forgot to be a paleontologist when I grew up!" In the next exercises, you will explore things that you forgot to become, too. Or maybe you didn't forget, but felt your dreams were impractical or impossible. Maybe you worried that pursuing your interests would leave you open to judgment or rejection, or you needed encouragement that wasn't available.

Now is a great time to revisit those abandoned interests to see if they still hold a spark. You have acquired additional life skills and added discipline to pursue your interests. You're less likely to be derailed by the need for acceptance. You can explore what lights you up, following your intuition and your gut.

As you do these exercises, write down every thought, no matter how insignificant it may initially seem. You never know where ideas will lead, and what will be the seed that takes root and flourishes.

BLAST FROM THE PAST

When you were a kid, how did you love to play? Did you like dressing up and pretending? Exploring? Solving puzzles? Painting? Making blanket forts? Did you like playing with one or two best friends, or was it fun to be part of a bigger group?

_____

_____

_____

_____

_____

_____

_____

_____

_____

_____

_____

_____

_____

_____

_____

WHAT ARE YOU WEARING?

As a therapist, I wear loose, comfy clothes. I half joke that it's why I chose my second career. What do you see yourself wearing in your ideal life? Steel-toed boots? A chef's apron? A power suit? What would it feel like to dress your ideal way on a daily basis?

_____

_____

_____

_____

_____

_____

_____

_____

_____

_____

_____

_____

_____

_____

_____

_____

THE WONDERFUL DAY

Imagine a day with no obligations and nothing on your to-do list. Ask yourself, "What would feel wonderful to do today?" Do you want to be inside or out? Do you want to be active, or would it feel good to rest and read, listen to music, or watch television? Do you want to spend time with others? Who? Would you rather be alone? What would you do if no one was watching and you didn't have anyone else to take into consideration? Use this space to tell the story of the Wonderful Day.

_____

_____

_____

_____

_____

_____

_____

_____

_____

_____

_____

_____

_____

TRUST YOUR INTUITION

Intuition is not magical thinking. It's part of implicit learning—when you know something without remembering how you learned it. Trusting your gut allows you to make good choices when logic says otherwise. Write about a time when you followed an intuition with good results—or discovered you should have.

_____

_____

_____

_____

_____

_____

_____

_____

_____

_____

_____

_____

_____

_____

I follow my curiosity and sense of wonder. I trust my intuition and my gut to tell me when I'm on the right path.

IDENTIFYING WHAT DOESN'T WORK FOR YOU

Write about your pet peeves and irritations. Knowing what you don't want to experience will help you avoid or weed out situations, personality types, and environments you already know don't work for you. Do this exercise with abandon. Hate fluorescent lighting? Write it down.

1. _____

2. _____

3. _____

4. _____

5. _____

6. _____

7. _____

8. _____

9. _____

10. _____

The Best Part of Waking Up

Many of us wake up to an alarm. Ugh, that word alone is stressful. Alarms are for fires and burglars! Once that alarm goes off, we either fight with ourselves over staying in bed or we fling ourselves into the daily grind. Yuck. You are creating a future you love, so why not become someone you love waking up to?

1. Find the best tone or music to wake up to. Or experiment with a light that comes on gradually to wake you.

2. For the next three days, see how it feels to take those first few moments to just be with yourself in a warm, friendly way. While you're still in bed, gently stretch if that feels good. Give yourself a hug—real or imaginary. You can use a pillow if it helps.

3. Set an intention for the day, something that is just for you, for your own happiness and well-being. An example might be the intention to notice something beautiful before the end of the day or to find something that makes you laugh. If you tend to wake up groggy, set this intention the night before and review it in the morning.

   Imagine how you would feel if you engaged in this practice every morning.

A YEAR TO LIVE

Imagine you have one year left to live, one more birthday, one more New Year's Eve. This process can help you focus on what really matters. Take this exercise month by month. Who would you spend time with first? Last? What parts of the world would you visit in different seasons? What would you stop doing? Is there a legacy you'd want to leave behind? How would you treat yourself and others? What becomes more urgent or important and what becomes less serious or necessary when you have only a year left?

_____

_____

_____

_____

_____

_____

_____

_____

_____

_____

_____

_____

I AM THE KIND OF PERSON WHO . . .

This exercise helps not just with self-awareness but also being true to yourself. Once completed, you can use it to unapologetically communicate your needs and preferences. List everything you know about yourself by finishing each of the following sentences.

1. I am the kind of person who _____

_____

_____

2. I am the kind of person who _____

_____

_____

3. I am the kind of person who _____

_____

_____

4. I am the kind of person who _____

_____

_____

5. I am the kind of person who _____

_____

_____

CONSTANT AS THE NORTHERN STAR

It's natural for your tastes and interests to evolve and change as you grow. But often there are a few keystones in personalities and preferences that remain constant. Looking back, what are your constants? A love of corny jokes? A fascination with the Olympics? How do these constant keystones contribute to your life?

_____

_____

_____

_____

_____

_____

_____

_____

_____

_____

_____

_____

WHOM DO YOU ADMIRE?

The traits we admire in others are often traits we want to cultivate. I admire my friend Shauna because she accepts herself with warmth and humor. I admire the writer Anne Lamott for similar reasons. I clearly value self-acceptance and humor in myself and others.

Write about three people you admire. What do you admire about them? Why? How have they impacted your life? List any traits that they have in common. Those are likely traits you want to bring out in yourself. How can you develop them?

_____

_____

_____

_____

_____

_____

_____

_____

_____

_____

_____

_____

Calming Your Inner Critic

Think of your inner critic as a teenager whose job is making sure you fit in and look cool. No matter how wise or mature you become, your inner critic can show up and shut you down, especially if you want to do something that feels new, challenging, or vulnerable. This exercise will give you a healthy and safe way to work on confronting, reducing, or eliminating the fear your critic uses to keep you from taking risks.

1. When you notice your inner critic being activated, write down the criticisms and mean things it says. Example: "I've been playing guitar for months and I still sound terrible."

2. In the next column, write down the underlying fear. Example: "I'm afraid I'll never be good enough."

3. Then write down how you will protect yourself from that fear. Example: "I'm playing for the pleasure of learning. I don't have to impress anyone. And playing just because I like it means I will be more likely to practice. I probably will get better with time. Either way, I'm okay."

INNER CRITIC	UNDERLYING FEAR	PROTECTION FROM THE FEAR

INTROVERT OR EXTROVERT?

Extroverts get energy from other people. Introverts need solitude to recharge. Do you get your energy from others or from solitude? How do you know when you need company or alone time? What signals in your body or mood help you know when to reach out or pull back?

_____

_____

_____

_____

_____

_____

_____

_____

_____

_____

_____

_____

_____

_____

_____

_____

I am becoming more comfortable in my own skin. I honor who I am. My way is the right way for me.

I HIGHLY RECOMMEND . . . ME!

We get used to being who we are and knowing what we know, so we may not realize our experiences and perspectives make us special, unique, and valuable. In this exercise, write a recommendation for yourself as though you were a favorite employee. Even if you haven't had a traditional job, you've certainly done your share of work by this point in life. Include intangible qualities like spotting opportunities others don't see or bringing out the best in others. Wax poetic about how wonderful you are. If necessary, send your inner critic out for coffee.

_____

_____

_____

_____

_____

_____

_____

_____

_____

_____

_____

_____

_____

_____

CHANGING THE WORLD

If you had the power to instantly change the world, what would you change? How? Write down at least three things, both personal and global. What does your list tell you about your values and ideals?

_____

_____

_____

_____

_____

_____

_____

_____

_____

_____

_____

_____

_____

_____

_____

My happiness and satisfaction are a gift to myself and to the world. I am a role model for living a meaningful life.

FINDING FLOW

When you're so immersed in work that you lose track of time or forget to eat, you're in a state of flow. It's deeply fulfilling. Recalling times you have felt flow can help you rediscover your passions.

Write about three times you've experienced flow. What were you doing? Who were you with? What was the environment like—lighting, sounds, and smells? What were you working on? How did you become involved in the project or activity? What did you learn? What made the activity feel so engaging? What passions do recalling these experiences reveal?

_____

_____

_____

_____

_____

_____

_____

_____

_____

_____

_____

_____

PART 2

Find the Joy You Already Have

Celebration is a powerful practice for creating and sustaining motivation. The following exercises will help you savor your joys and accomplishments. Taking time to delight in the things you love will also prime your brain to recognize what will bring you joy going forward.

Reflecting on your successes can also foster resilience when facing new challenges. When I started my private practice, I asked former colleagues and supervisors to email me with the things they appreciated about working with me. I have saved those emails, as well as thank-you notes from clients over the years. I reread them whenever I feel unsteady.

As you create a life you love, you can reread this journal, maybe specifically this section, whenever you need a confidence boost or a reminder that you have already accomplished so much. Get ready to be in awe of your wonderful self.

WELLSPRINGS

A wellspring is a bountiful source of something. Finding the wellsprings in your life is tremendously beneficial. What sustains you and feeds your soul? Relationships? Work? Hobbies? A self-care practice? I love gardening, cooking, and cleaning. I love the sense of accomplishment when a project is done. How do your wellsprings impact your happiness?

_____

_____

_____

_____

_____

_____

_____

_____

_____

_____

_____

_____

_____

PRIDE AND JOY

Looking back over your life, make a list of all your accomplishments, big or small, personal or professional. If there are things you feel proud of that have mattered only to you, they count, too. Example: "I'm really proud of finding an exercise routine I can stick to."

_____

_____

_____

_____

_____

_____

_____

_____

_____

_____

_____

_____

_____

_____

AMPLIFY THE GOOD #1

In therapy, I use a process called amplification. When you take time to focus on experiences and feelings you enjoy, those good feelings become stronger. I ask clients to amplify the good at every opportunity. Here is your opportunity to do the same.

Choose three accomplishments from the last exercise you feel most proud of. Write about each in depth. Why does it feel good? Has it made a difference for you and/or others? How has it changed you or helped you grow?

_____

_____

_____

_____

_____

_____

_____

_____

_____

_____

_____

_____

_____

I APPRECIATE YOU

When we experience genuine gratitude, it feels wonderful. Make a gratitude list below. After each item or relationship, write a few words about how it makes a difference in your life. Then pause and notice how it feels to be in appreciation. Thinking about the feeling will help you amplify it.

_____

_____

_____

_____

_____

_____

_____

_____

_____

_____

_____

_____

_____

_____

When I feel joy, I know I'm on the right path. Creating, embracing, and celebrating joy gives my life meaning and purpose.

DID I DO THAT?

I was sick with nerves before my licensing exams. But when I found out I passed, I felt bullet-proof. I didn't just master the test materials; I conquered my own fear. Write about a time when your own strength, skill, or ability surprised you.

_____

_____

_____

_____

_____

_____

_____

_____

_____

_____

_____

_____

_____

_____

_____

Collect Joy

There's a famous saying: "What you pay attention to grows." How wonderful that you can direct your attention wherever you want. Take a moment now and look for anything that gives you joy. If you feel stuck, focus on little things—the smell of baked goods or getting a great price on something you need. You may have to build up this muscle.

I love walking through my neighborhood and noticing how people decorate their homes and plant their gardens. You might find that a friendly waiter gives you joy. Or seeing kids running through sprinklers on a hot day. Power tip: Creating joy for others can also give you joy.

Become a collector of joy. For the next three days, notice which activities, people, places, and things—even which of your own thoughts—bring you joy. If you find this practice helpful, consider making it an ongoing habit. You are cultivating the power to create moments of happiness, no matter what else may be going on. Collecting joy alone will add meaning to your life. The next time someone asks what you do, you can say, "I am a joy collector." You might start a trend.

THE POWER OF KINDNESS

Kindness can improve mental and physical health. Whether you are the giver, the receiver, or a witness to kindness, you still receive the benefits, including improved self-esteem and cardio-vascular health.

How do you define kindness? Think about a time when you received a kindness that made a difference. Write the story of what happened and how it made you feel. Then write about a time when you gave a kindness or witnessed a kindness. Tell that story. Finally, write about the feelings you notice now, as you remember these experiences.

_____

_____

_____

_____

_____

_____

_____

_____

_____

_____

_____

_____

JOY IN MOTION

The mind-body connection flows in both directions. Movement can foster joy. Exercise releases endorphins. Smiling releases happy neurotransmitters. Watching a great dancer or athlete can feel good, too. Write about a time when you enjoyed watching or participating in physical activity. How did movement bring you joy?

_____

_____

_____

_____

_____

_____

_____

_____

_____

_____

_____

_____

_____

_____

ONLY CONNECT

Write about three people who bring joy to your life. You may share a sense of humor, a well of compassion, a sense of unconditional love, or a shared interest. They may be family, chosen family, or friends. Describe in detail what you love about each person.

_____

_____

_____

_____

_____

_____

_____

_____

_____

_____

_____

_____

_____

_____

APPLAUD YOUR COURAGE

It takes guts to get to middle age. You've endured relationship troubles, job changes, and losses. Something inside you helped you find the courage, strength, and resilience to keep going. Maybe you have a spiritual practice that sustains you. Maybe you've created a support network that strengthens you. Maybe it's your connection to nature or a self-belief that's unshakable.

Write about the times in your life when you had to be courageous. What got you through? How does it feel now to know you made it?

_____

_____

_____

_____

_____

_____

_____

_____

_____

_____

_____

_____

_____

_____

_____

_____

_____

_____

_____

_____

_____

_____

_____

_____

_____

_____

_____

_____

_____

I FEEL GOOD WHEN . . .

Joy often presents itself in small ways that you can easily miss if you're not tuned in. The next exercise can help jump-start your sense of mindfulness about small, simple things that make you feel good. It can be especially helpful if you have difficulty identifying joy in your life. You can replace the word "good" with another word that works better for you (such as joy, ease, relief, peace, comfort, or happiness).

I feel good when I am wearing _____

I feel good when I read about _____

I feel good when I am with _____

I feel good when I listen to _____

I feel good when I am surrounded by _____

I feel good when I eat _____

I feel good when I think about _____

I feel good when I'm in places like _____

I feel good when I'm working on _____

I feel good when I can just relax and _____

CREATIVITY

Kids are creative. They pretend to be pirates. They draw and paint. They make up silly songs and sing into spoon-microphones. How are you creative as an adult? You may write or play an instrument. Or you may scrounge up wild Halloween costumes. How do you feed your creative soul?

_____

_____

_____

_____

_____

_____

_____

_____

_____

_____

_____

_____

_____

_____

I can focus on joy, past and present, whenever I want. I have the power to create my own joy. I am a joy collector.

TIME TRAVEL

Think about a time when you didn't yet know who you were or what you were capable of. Imagine time traveling back to that younger self. Talk about everything wonderful that's going to happen—adventures, successes, interesting people you meet, and things you learn. If doing so is difficult, think about the support or encouragement you needed at the time. What did you need to hear to follow your heart? Write what you said to yourself. Then write what it felt like for your younger self to get this preview/encouragement.

THE LITTLE THINGS

Small things, added up over time, often make life feel joyful. Maybe it's the taste of perfectly ripe summer fruit or the way your cat's tongue hangs out when he's sleeping. Today, notice the little things that make you happy, content, or satisfied. List those things below.

_____

_____

_____

_____

_____

_____

_____

_____

_____

_____

_____

_____

_____

_____

_____

Filling my own cup with joy allows me to be more present for others. When I feel good, I do good. My joy is contagious.

AMPLIFY THE GOOD #2

Read through your entries in this section. How does it feel to reexperience the joy you've created or felt in different areas and at different times in your life? Imagine amplifying any good feelings in your mind and body, making them bigger and stronger.

What have you learned about your happiness, accomplishments, relationships, and satisfaction that you hadn't thought about before? As you create meaning and purpose in the next stages of life, how will joy factor in? How can you make joy a guiding principle going forward?

_____

_____

_____

_____

_____

_____

_____

_____

_____

_____

_____

_____

_____

_____

PART 3

Appreciate What You've Learned

Finding purpose in midlife can feel daunting, but you come to this transition with a wealth of experience. Though you may be moving in a new direction, you already know what it's like to be new. You know that the new feeling will pass before long. You know that fear of the unknown melts as you begin taking steps, each one leading to the next, until you find your destination.

In this section, you will explore the experiences and lessons you bring to this transitional time and beyond. You will find the touchstones within you—those aspects of your personality and experience that remain constant, even as you make changes. You will ground yourself in your wisdom and the lessons you have already learned. This grounding will help you feel more secure as you think about any changes you want to embrace going forward.

THE GIFTS OF MATURITY

A mature mind is a wonderful thing. It's a relief to get past the drama and impulsivity of youth, and your mature mind is your greatest asset during this transition. How do you define maturity? What gifts has maturity given you? What are you still working on?

_____

_____

_____

_____

_____

_____

_____

_____

_____

_____

_____

_____

_____

_____

_____

_____

THE UNIVERSITY OF LIFE

I like to think of mistakes as the tuition paid to the University of Life. Regrets help us avoid pain, embarrassment, headaches, and heartache. List five of your mistakes, big or small. Then write down the lessons you learned from each experience.

_____

_____

_____

_____

_____

_____

_____

_____

_____

_____

_____

_____

_____

_____

_____

_____

_____

FORGIVING YOURSELF

To embrace lessons you've learned from your mistakes, you might need to practice self-forgiveness. It means reestablishing trust that you won't make the same mistakes again.

Looking over your list on the previous page, choose one or two mistakes that still feel embarrassing, frustrating, or difficult to resolve. First, write yourself a heartfelt apology for making the mistake. Then delve deeper into the lessons you learned. What is the risk you might make the same mistake? How will you avoid that risk? How have you earned (or will you earn) your trust again?

_____

_____

_____

_____

_____

_____

_____

_____

_____

_____

_____

_____

SEE HOW FAR YOU'VE COME

Write about a skill, a perspective, or a practice you've worked hard to cultivate. For example, "I'm proud of my self-acceptance because it was hard won." What's your skill? How did you manage it? What qualities did you develop that will help with future challenges?

_____

_____

_____

_____

_____

_____

_____

_____

_____

_____

_____

_____

_____

_____

_____

_____

_____

I am always evolving, so I will forgive my mistakes. They are a normal part of self-discovery. I celebrate what I've learned and welcome future growth.

THE DIFFICULT PERSON

Great villains make great heroes. The villain's treachery compels the hero to become more resourceful and overcome the odds in creative, compelling ways. Write about a difficult person who made you stronger, smarter, or better equipped in some way.

_____

_____

_____

_____

_____

_____

_____

_____

_____

_____

_____

_____

_____

_____

_____

_____

_____

Recognition

We tend to dismiss or discount our own efforts. In this exercise, you will take time to appreciate your work—mental, physical, emotional, or spiritual. Recognition improves morale, motivation, and perseverance—qualities that can help you cultivate deep and lasting satisfaction.

1. Find a quiet place where you can sit comfortably without interruption for about 10 minutes.

2. Think about some effort in your life that you feel good about, such as overcoming a fear or mastering a skill.

3. Reflect on what you had to do to make that effort successful. Did you let go of self-limiting beliefs? Find your courage? Make sacrifices?

4. How did that experience change you? How did it impact your choices or perspectives? How has it empowered you or changed your self-image?

5. Placing your hands over your heart and closing your eyes, send appreciation, kudos, and gratitude to the person you were, who took the steps you took and made that moment happen. Allow yourself to go deep here. Imagine receiving an award from an organization or person you respect and admire. Feel the appreciation in your whole body.

Repeat this process whenever you need to feel appreciated or want a boost in self-confidence.

HONORING YOUR TEACHERS

Write a thank-you letter to someone who has helped you become more of the person you want to be. It can be an actual teacher or someone who modeled a way of thinking or behaving you admired and emulated. What did they teach you about yourself? What did you learn about the world or other people? What qualities did they draw out in you? What do you value most about that relationship? How do you carry this person in your heart or mind today?

_____

_____

_____

_____

_____

_____

_____

_____

_____

_____

_____

_____

_____

_____

NEW TRICKS FOR US SWEET OLD DOGS

Age itself is a powerful teacher. Many of us learn that we must take better care of our muscles and joints, our mental health, and our relationships with others to maintain a high quality of life. What has growing older taught you?

_____

_____

_____

_____

_____

_____

_____

_____

_____

_____

_____

_____

_____

_____

_____

SELF-IMAGE

Self-image encompasses the ideas you have about your abilities, appearance, and personality. Sometimes self-image is distorted by negative experiences. List some words you'd use to describe yourself, good and bad. How did you get each label? Do you agree with it? Is it something you like or want to change?

_____

_____

_____

_____

_____

_____

_____

_____

_____

_____

_____

_____

_____

_____

_____

SO MUCH IN COMMON

Imagine meeting someone at a party and discovering you have a lot in common. You love the same movies and music. You find the same things funny, weird, or irritating. The more you talk, the more you discover you share, including values, opinions, and aspirations. Answer the following questions about meeting this person.

What is it like to meet someone so similar, someone who really gets you?

_____

_____

How do you feel about them? Do you want to spend more time with them?

_____

_____

Of course, this person is you. What is it like to see yourself through this lens?

_____

_____

_____

_____

_____

_____

_____

_____

_____

_____

_____

_____

_____

_____

_____

_____

_____

_____

_____

_____

_____

_____

_____

_____

_____

_____

Self-Love vs. Self-Esteem

Love and esteem are two routes to the sense of value and belonging we all need.

Self-esteem suggests respect and confidence, which must be earned over and over again. Seeking esteem, we tend to look outside ourselves for validation, vulnerable to the opinions and whims of others who may have their own agendas.

Self-love can be generated without anyone else. Engaging in kind, gentle actions (like feeding yourself delicious, wholesome food or taking breaks when you feel tired), along with speaking to yourself in a warm, friendly way (instead of in frustration or self-criticism), can make you feel more loved.

I tell my clients: "It's not being good enough that wins us love. It's being loved for no reason that, in the end, makes us feel good enough."

In the left column below, write down five practices you can develop to make yourself feel loved. Then answer the question "Why do I need this?" in the right column.

LOVING PRACTICES	WHY DO I NEED THIS?

CHERISHING YOURSELF

Building on the last exercise, write a letter to your future self explaining why you are creating a life you love. Describe how your future joy might ease past struggles and why your happiness matters. Write as though you love yourself deeply.

_____

_____

_____

_____

_____

_____

_____

_____

_____

_____

_____

_____

_____

_____

_____

RESPONSIBILITY

Eleanor Roosevelt said, "With freedom comes responsibility." I think the reverse is true, too. List three ways you've gained freedom or personal power by taking responsibility for yourself. For example, taking financial responsibility can free you from anxiety about your future. How does it feel to be taking responsibility for your future happiness through this journal?

_____

_____

_____

_____

_____

_____

_____

_____

_____

_____

_____

_____

_____

_____

*I am grateful for everything I've learned
and the work I've done to get here.*

*Every experience I've had has contributed
to my knowledge, skill, and wisdom.*

WHAT'S YOUR MASTER CLASS?

Imagine you've been invited to teach a master class on a topic or process you love. Don't worry about what others may think of your topic. Maybe you're a genius at making playlists for parties. Maybe you are a container-garden artist. Just make sure you can share not only how to do it but also why it's so interesting or valuable.

What would you teach and why? How did you gain your mastery? Why does this topic fascinate you? What would you want people to learn from you?

_____

_____

_____

_____

_____

_____

_____

_____

_____

_____

_____

_____

_____

PRIORITIES

One of the best things about being older is knowing how much we can get done, how long things really take, and what is important. What have you learned over the years about your priorities? How have they evolved? What would you like to prioritize more?

_____

_____

_____

_____

_____

_____

_____

_____

_____

_____

_____

_____

_____

_____

_____

_____

_____

I use my knowledge and self-awareness to create a life I love. My choices, preferences, and needs reflect everything I have learned.

YOUR INNER COMPASS

Our values inform our decisions, whether we spend or save, who we admire, and when to prioritize the needs of others versus ourselves. Values are passed down in families and institutions. Sometimes those values deepen as we see their wisdom. Sometimes we outgrow them.

Imagine you are mentoring someone younger. What would you tell them is the singular most important value in life? How do they learn it? Will it change over time? If so, how?

_____

_____

_____

_____

_____

_____

_____

_____

_____

_____

_____

_____

_____

_____

PART 4

See the World Anew

In childhood, we are naturally curious and optimistic. We believe in magic and pretend we are astronauts, scientists, singers, and acrobats. These options feel entirely possible as we imagine ourselves the heroes of our own stories.

Then culture, family, and fear convince us to avoid risks that might lead to failure or embarrassment. It's time to assess whether those risks are actually dangerous. Maybe now you can tolerate being new and looking a little dorky. Maybe the concerns or judgments of others don't matter as much.

In this section, you will explore the possibility of expanding your comfort zone, reclaiming the wonder and optimism of childhood. If, as author Jack Canfield writes, "Everything you want is on the other side of fear," then it's time to practice giving yourself the en-COURAGE-ment you need to take some risks and reap the rewards.

DAYDREAM BELIEVER

What were your daydreams as a kid or teenager? Did you love peering through the lens of a microscope, imagining life as a scientist? Did you see yourself playing guitar in a punk rock band? What are your more recent daydreams?

_____

_____

_____

_____

_____

_____

_____

_____

_____

_____

_____

_____

_____

_____

_____

_____

WHAT'S GETTING IN THE WAY?

Thinking about the daydreams in the last exercise, did you notice any negativity come up? It's important to know what stops you so you can shift self-limiting beliefs. Write down any fears or negative thoughts about your dreams.

_____

_____

_____

_____

_____

_____

_____

_____

_____

_____

_____

_____

_____

_____

_____

REFRAMING

You can overcome self-limiting beliefs by reframing or looking at a situation from another angle.

Example:

Belief: It's selfish to focus on my needs.

Reframe: Taking care of my needs gives me energy to help others.

Belief: I feel too old to learn new things.

Reframe: Learning new things protects the brain from cognitive decline.

Belief: If I disappoint others, I will pay a price.

Reframe: Most people can tolerate disappointment. I can spend less time with anyone punitive.

Reframe your self-limiting beliefs.

_____

_____

_____

_____

_____

_____

_____

_____

_____

_____

_____

_____

_____

_____

_____

_____

_____

_____

_____

_____

_____

_____

_____

_____

_____

_____

_____

IF I HAD NO FEAR . . .

If you didn't have the fears or concerns you listed in the "What's Getting in the Way?" exercise (see page 81), what would you do? How would you be different? Where would you go? What interests would you delve into? Who would you want to meet?

If I had no fear I would _____

_____

_____

If I had no fear I would _____

_____

_____

If I had no fear I would _____

_____

_____

I embrace curiosity and wonder, inviting new experiences with an open heart and open mind; I gently and persistently expand my comfort zone day by day.

FIND YOUR TRIBE

I love the phrase "The weirdness in me honors the weirdness in you." When you leave your comfort zone, it helps for you to have a tribe of like-minded people. What qualities do your ideal tribe members share? What do you geek-out on together? Who would welcome the weirdness in you?

_____

_____

_____

_____

_____

_____

_____

_____

_____

_____

_____

_____

_____

_____

_____

_____

Finding Inspiration

Sometimes it's helpful for you to get out of your own head and find inspiration elsewhere. Blogs, TED Talks, YouTube tutorials, documentaries, and online courses are available on almost any topic. Just browsing what's accessible online can give you ideas.

You might also find inspiration by perusing social media groups to see what others are doing. You may find inspiration through your local rec and parks or community center. Some libraries offer classes, events, and speakers, too.

1. Using one of the resources listed above (or another if you prefer), browse through the courses or activities available. Notice what sparks your interest or curiosity. Don't concern yourself at this point with feasibility. You are just getting ideas about topics that interest you.

2. Start a list of ideas to explore. Add to this list over time, whenever you discover something intriguing.

3. Talk to people who are already taking a class, in a group, or practicing something that piques your interest. Ask how they got involved and what they like most about the topic.

4. See if there's an introductory class or meeting, something to try without commitment. If you enjoy it, you may decide to delve further.

DISMANTLING CULTURAL CONSTRAINTS

Reclaiming awe and wonder may mean rejecting limiting beliefs you've absorbed through socialization. These beliefs often center around gender norms, morality, avoiding judgment, and being "good" or pleasing others. Fortunately, critical thinking can help you assess and reject any "norms" that hold you back.

Imagine you are at a roundtable with your tribe, discussing the familial, religious, cultural, or societal beliefs you've internalized. Who is at the table? What are their beliefs? Which do you share? Which ones are no longer working for you? What has changed inside of you or in the world that makes these beliefs obsolete?

_____

_____

_____

_____

_____

_____

_____

_____

_____

_____

_____

_____

LOVE IT/LOATHE IT

Strong feelings help pinpoint the things we need more and less of in our lives. I love it when I take a midday nap and gain a burst of energy. I loathe it when I'm on a creative roll and something distracts me. What are your loves and loathes?

I LOVED IT WHEN	I LOATHED IT WHEN

I WANT MORE! MORE! MORE!

Looking at your loves in the previous exercise, what can you start doing now to make them a bigger part of your life? What do you want more of daily? Weekly? Monthly? How can you make space for these things? What resources or support do you need to make it happen?

_____

_____

_____

_____

_____

_____

_____

_____

_____

_____

_____

_____

_____

_____

BOUNDARIES

A common limiting belief is that you will get in trouble if you disappoint others. It can stop you from setting boundaries.

Considering the time and energy needed to pursue your dreams—to explore, develop skills, travel, or take classes—what activities do you need to limit? Consult your list of "loathes."

Imagine setting these boundaries. Who would you say no to? How do you want to convey the message? What might get in the way of saying no?

Pro tip: To gain confidence, practice on someone likely to be understanding.

_____

_____

_____

_____

_____

_____

_____

_____

_____

_____

_____

_____

Setting Intentions

In this exercise, you will use intentions to discover what you want to experience in nine aspects of your life. Use the space below to identify one intention for each aspect, an action to fulfill that intention, and a reason the intention is important.

Physical

Intention: _____

One Easy Action: _____

Importance: _____

Emotional

Intention: _____

One Easy Action: _____

Importance: _____

Financial

Intention: _____

One Easy Action: _____

Importance: _____

Social

Intention: _____

One Easy Action: _____

Importance: _____

Spiritual

Intention: _____

One Easy Action: _____

Importance: _____

Romantic

Intention: _____

One Easy Action: _____

Importance: _____

Familial

Intention: _____

One Easy Action: _____

Importance: _____

Recreational

Intention: _____

One Easy Action: _____

Importance: _____

Professional

Intention: _____

One Easy Action: _____

Importance: _____

THE FEELING OF ACCOMPLISHMENT

Thinking about the previous exercise, write about how your life will be different when you have fulfilled your intentions. Knowing the feeling you want to achieve can help with flexibility. If you don't meet the goal but find another way to create the same feeling, then you've met your intention.

_____

_____

_____

_____

_____

_____

_____

_____

_____

_____

_____

_____

_____

_____

I hold my interests sacred, knowing my curiosity points me to a life I love. I carefully protect the time I need to explore and grow.

INTERNSHIP

Imagine you have a year of "internships"—situations where you can explore whatever you want and then move on. Choose four you would like to do in a year. They can be personal or professional. You might spend time on an archaeological dig, volunteering for a cause that's dear to you, or reading manuscripts for a literary agency.

Write about each internship. What do you want to learn from each one? What if it was your life? Would you like it? Why or why not?

_____

_____

_____

_____

_____

_____

_____

_____

_____

_____

_____

_____

_____

_____

BE YOUR OWN GUIDE

When you do something new, it's helpful for you to have a guide. At times when you don't have a mentor, how can you become your own guide? What words of encouragement would help you stay on track? What books, podcasts, or other resources could you use to give yourself more guidance?

_____

_____

_____

_____

_____

_____

_____

_____

_____

_____

_____

_____

_____

_____

I explore my interests without pressuring myself. I listen to my gut and invite more of what feels enlivening while letting go of anything that doesn't serve me.

FEAR OF THE UNKNOWN

Fear of the unknown signals a lack of trust in yourself. But if you've made it to midlife, you can clearly take care of yourself, even when life surprises you.

Imagine you are writing your memoir. Tell your readers how you managed three different times life took you by surprise. What inner resources did you discover? Who showed up to help? How did those experiences make you stronger or wiser? What actions or words of encouragement helped you navigate? As you write, does your self-trust deepen?

_____

_____

_____

_____

_____

_____

_____

_____

_____

_____

_____

_____

_____

PART 5

Light Your Creative Fire

Creativity is about finding patterns, being curious, asking questions, solving problems, experimenting, and synthesizing ideas. Whether your future lies in the arts, in business, or in serving the greater good, your creativity will be an asset.

As you build a future you love, creative thinking will help you find connections and insights. Accessing your creative spirit may also inspire you to explore forms of self-expression you find rich and rewarding. Even if you don't consider yourself "creative," you can find joy in the development of creative skills.

This section will help you practice and train your creative skills and hone your creative thinking. Think of it as a form of play. Have fun. Invite your inner child to come out. Let your imagination have free rein. All those things you said you would do later, when you had more time? Now is that time. You are in your prime. Dive in!

If your inner critic gets activated, use the "Calming Your Inner Critic" exercise (see page 16) to identify and comfort the fear underlying the criticism.

WOW!

In this exercise, you will use free association to create an image that inspires you (maybe one you could print on T-shirts and sell!). Fill the space below with words, phrases, and ideas that make you say wow. Play with printing, handwriting, colored pens, all caps, or different-size letters.

WONDERLAND

Creativity dries up in cynicism. Wonder revives it. Take a moment to marvel at something within 10 feet of you right now. It could be a gadget. Your shoes. Reading glasses. Write down what's wonderful about this object or marvelous about how it came to be.

_____

_____

_____

_____

_____

_____

_____

_____

_____

_____

_____

_____

_____

_____

_____

TWEAK THAT!

Some of the best creative ideas are improvements on designs that already exist: heated car seats, travel wear with hidden pockets, multicookers, etc.

Imagine you are hired to improve on an existing design. Think about a tool, gadget, or garment you almost love. How would you improve it? Write a proposal for creating this improvement. Describe the need it would fulfill. Why would your tweak make the existing tool easier to use or more effective? Who would buy this product? Why do they need it?

_____

_____

_____

_____

_____

_____

_____

_____

_____

_____

_____

_____

_____

_____

ASPIRATIONS

Aspirations are bigger than goals. The word shares a root with "spirit." It suggests a yearning, maybe one that persists over time. If nothing could stop you, what would you aspire to be or do? Why does this feel important or exciting?

_____

_____

_____

_____

_____

_____

_____

_____

_____

_____

_____

_____

_____

_____

_____

I am a creative person. I am guided by wonder, curiosity, and awe. I seek opportunities to make the world a better and more beautiful place.

CONSTRAINTS

Limitations can help our creative spirit. For example, I've had to learn how to prepare meals without salt or sugar to cook for family members with health concerns. These constraints pushed me to become more creative, trying new ingredients and experimenting with recipes. Write about a time when a constraint made you more creative or innovative.

_____

_____

_____

_____

_____

_____

_____

_____

_____

_____

_____

_____

_____

_____

_____

Zone Out on Purpose

Our brains turn to mush when we work too long. It's when we allow ourselves to do nothing for a while that the best ideas and solutions seem to come to us. One of my favorite science writers, Dan Hurley, says mind-wandering can be a powerful tool for problem-solving or creative thinking. I agree. Take time during each of the next three days to let your mind wander.

1. Schedule at least 10 minutes of uninterrupted time.

2. Choose something mindless to do. Having options in advance can help so you don't have to come up with ideas when your brain is tired. These can include:

   - Walking outdoors (no phone!)
   - Doodling
   - Taking a shower
   - Puttering (straightening your desk, organizing your socks, etc.)
   - Napping
   - Staring out a window

   _____

   _____

   _____

3. Allow yourself to let go of any "shoulds" or "musts" during this time. Remind yourself you are doing "nothing" on purpose. This is not wasted time. It's an experiment.

4. Notice what happens when you zone out. Do ideas come to you? What happens in the hours that follow? Are you more refreshed? Clear-headed?

SHIFTING PERSPECTIVE

Art students learn to draw by turning the image they are reproducing upside down. Instead of a specific object, they just see colors, shapes, and lines. Removing context shifts how you perceive and interpret patterns. It makes the brain more flexible and adaptable.

1. Find a photo or an image from a magazine.

2. Turn it upside down.

3. Quickly sketch what you see—just shapes and lines—in the space below.

4. Were you able to let go of what it was supposed to look like? Or did you try to capture the image? What do you think this exercise says about you?

_____

_____

_____

5. What would happen if you looked at the world "upside down" in other situations? Where do you feel like you most need a new perspective?

_____

_____

_____

THIS IS NOT (JUST) A FORK

Building on upside-down drawing, let's continue shifting perspective. Find an everyday object, like a fork or scarf, and write down seven things you could do with it besides its intended use. Get creative! These ideas don't need to be practical; the exercise is about a shift in thinking.

1. _____

2. _____

3. _____

4. _____

5. _____

6. _____

7. _____

YOUR MIDLIFE SOUNDTRACK

The right song can transport you in time, evoke any emotion, and bring your energy up or down. Imagine scoring the movie of your future story. Thinking about a future you love and the feelings you want to have, what songs make up the soundtrack of your life?

1. _____

2. _____

3. _____

4. _____

5. _____

6. _____

7. _____

EMPATHY

Empathy is the heart of creative expression. Artists in every medium create emotional experiences for audiences. The desire to ease pain and create comfort leads to innovation in every field. In this exercise, you will explore creativity while engaging empathy.

Write a short story about a day in the life of a sentient houseplant. Does the plant look down on the "unrooted" who can't even synthesize their own food? Is it envious, wishing for legs? Does it like the people who water it? Is it getting the care it needs?

_____

_____

_____

_____

_____

_____

_____

_____

_____

_____

_____

_____

_____

Creativity Care Plan

Your creative spirit needs regular care and tending to flourish. Answer the following questions in order to plan how you will nurture your creativity.

1. Environment: Describe your ideal space for creating. Is it indoors? Out? What ambient noises or smells surround you? What tools are at hand?

   _____

   _____

2. Schedule: What are your ideal sleep hours? Work hours? Social hours? Zone out times?

   _____

   _____

3. People: Who are your mentors or collaborators? How can they best support you?

   _____

   _____

4. Movement: What kind of exercise feels right for your mind/body? What gives you energy? How do you like to work out stress and kinks?

   _____

   _____

5. Inspiration: Drawing from the "Finding Inspiration" exercise (see page 87), what are your sources of inspiration? What books, magazines, podcasts, blogs, or classes fill your creative cup?

_____

_____

6. Spirituality: What spiritual practices, if any, nourish you? How often and in what ways do you want to connect spiritually? Is it important to express spiritual ideas creatively through art, music, dance, etc.?

_____

_____

7. Resources: What do you need to have on hand to flourish? Premade meals? Art supplies? Enough savings to focus on your dreams?

_____

_____

I DEFINE BEAUTY AS . . .

Beauty is in the eye of the beholder. That's you. It means you get to define beauty on your own terms. List five situations, places, people, or objects where you see beauty that others might miss. Then, based on your list, write your definition of beauty.

I find beauty in _____

I find beauty in _____

I find beauty in _____

I find beauty in _____

I find beauty in _____

I define beauty as _____

I actively cultivate and nurture my creativity, knowing it nourishes my spirit, keeps my brain healthy, and makes life more fun.

A LETTER TO THE COMMITTEE

Imagine applying for a grant so you can take a year off to pursue a creative project. Write a letter to the awarding committee describing your project. Choose one or more places you would visit; for example, a retreat with a studio where you could work without interruptions or a tour of locations to photograph or film a documentary. Highlight all the ways this project will benefit others. Tell them why this project is a passion for you or the fulfillment of a dream.

_____

_____

_____

_____

_____

_____

_____

_____

_____

_____

_____

_____

_____

_____

_____

PERSONAL TASTE AND STYLE

Your creativity and self-expression might come through in what you enjoy having around you. Imagine having an unlimited budget to design a space, indoors or out, that makes you happy. Write about the furnishings, flooring, plants, shelves, artwork, and anything else that would fill your happy place.

_____

_____

_____

_____

_____

_____

_____

_____

_____

_____

_____

_____

_____

_____

_____

My style, taste, and perspective make me unique. I have a distinctive voice when I am true to myself. My truth resonates with others.

YOUR PERSONAL STORY

Authenticity and vulnerability are at the heart of the best stories, movies, music, and art. Imagine your creative project is finished, and you have been asked to give a talk focusing on the personal aspects of creating and launching your project. What motivated you to create your project? What inner and outer obstacles did you overcome to make it happen? How does this project reflect where you are in your life? How did you take care of yourself while you worked? Where did you find inspiration, encouragement, and support?

_____

_____

_____

_____

_____

_____

_____

_____

_____

_____

_____

_____

_____

PART 6

Build the Future You Want to Live

You're in the homestretch! In this part, you will use the work you've done to build on your strengths, let go of situations that don't serve you anymore, and start planning a future that's in alignment with who you are today and who you are becoming.

You will get a deeper sense of your own grounding—where you already feel solid and where you want to grow more "roots." You will take an honest and compassionate look at your current needs and responsibilities as well as your wishes and hopes, so you know where you want to put your energy and attention going forward. Then you will begin planning how you want to move forward to create the ideal balance of work, play, and rest.

As you write, let go of any "shoulds" that may arise. Trust that it is not selfish to be true to yourself.

CONTINUITY

What are the things you would never change about yourself or your life? Think about qualities you feel proud of, values or ideals that have remained constant or grown stronger over time, and interests that still captivate you. They are foundational elements you will keep or grow as you think about new pursuits.

_____

_____

_____

_____

_____

_____

_____

_____

_____

_____

_____

_____

_____

_____

_____

_____

RECLAIMING

What interests have you let go or put off that you want to bring back into your life? Why do they feel important? What makes it the right time to reengage? What got in the way before? What feels different now?

_____

_____

_____

_____

_____

_____

_____

_____

_____

_____

_____

_____

_____

SAYING NO

A big motivator in midlife is the realization that time is short. That awareness can motivate you to let go of anything that feels draining, distracting, or just not right for you.

Imagine being free of guilt or fear that saying no will end badly. If you knew others would not take it personally, what are three boundaries you would set?

_____

_____

_____

_____

_____

_____

_____

_____

_____

_____

_____

_____

_____

_____

_____

How might you set these boundaries now? What wording avoids shaming or blaming yourself or others? How can you convey that you care even though your attention is elsewhere?

_____

_____

_____

_____

_____

_____

_____

_____

_____

_____

_____

_____

_____

_____

_____

SELF-LOVE

It's kind and loving to create the life you want. It means someone inside you cares about your happiness. Imagine being a person who cares about you. Write out your vows—promises you make—describing what you will do to give yourself security, respect, kindness, fun, and whatever else you need.

_____

_____

_____

_____

_____

_____

_____

_____

_____

_____

_____

_____

_____

I am learning to cherish myself by creating a fulfilling life. Giving myself the care I need, and experiences I want, is an act of self-love.

CULTIVATE THE FEELINGS YOU WANT

What do you want to feel every day? Awe? Wonder? Mastery? Love? Excitement? Hope? Comfort? Kindness? What are you already doing that creates these feelings? What would you like to do more of? Less of? What would help you listen to and honor your feelings going forward?

_____

_____

_____

_____

_____

_____

_____

_____

_____

_____

_____

_____

_____

_____

Letting Go

Fretting over things we can't control—especially what other people say, do, or think—robs us of time and energy we need to focus on our dreams. If you worry about the opinions of others, you might stop yourself from doing what you really love. This is a mental exercise you can use whenever you have worries about being judged or disappointing others.

1. Imagine throwing yourself a retirement party. It's no longer your job to fret over other people's opinions.

2. Remind yourself that you can't control what others do. Then visualize handing the situation over to the universe or a higher power.

3. Remind yourself that retiring doesn't mean you don't care. You can feel empathy while recognizing you have no power over the situation.

4. Give yourself time to feel any grief that you can't change how others feel or behave. Accepting reality doesn't mean you have to like it.

5. Repeat this process whenever you catch yourself feeling angst, irritation, or worry over someone or something that isn't in your control.

You may need to repeat this exercise until you rewire your brain. Eventually, it will get easier to step away from situations that leave you feeling stuck, resentful, or helpless.

GROWN-UP SUMMER CAMP

You don't have to be productive or solve the world's problems if that's not your thing. You might find meaning through having more fun. Kids have a great time exploring different interests at summer camp, where they can play games, do crafts, explore, or focus on an interest like science.

Write about the perfect summer camp for yourself. What activities would be fun? Create a structure for each day of the week. How would it feel to have days or weeks devoted to recreation? How can you incorporate more fun into your future?

Mondays: _____

_____

_____

Tuesdays: _____

_____

_____

Wednesdays: _____

_____

_____

Thursdays: _____

_____

_____

Fridays: _____

_____

_____

Saturdays: _____

_____

_____

Sundays: _____

_____

_____

TALENT

There is a misconception that some people have talent and some don't. This falsehood discourages us from working at things that are difficult. Talent is really the drive and interest to persevere until we have mastery. What do you have the drive and interest to practice now? Why is it important?

_____

_____

_____

_____

_____

_____

_____

_____

_____

_____

_____

_____

_____

BECOMING YOUR TRUE SELF

As a kid, I liked writing. In my first career, I used my communication skills to teach. In my second career, I teach clients how to love themselves. Each step moved me closer to my true self. What's been your path to the real you? What are the next steps in that path?

_____

_____

_____

_____

_____

_____

_____

_____

_____

_____

_____

_____

_____

_____

_____

_____

PAIN POINTS

Distress can signal areas for growth and development. Maybe you have worked at a job you disliked to make ends meet. Your intention might be figuring out how to earn a living doing something better.

Think about your sacrifices and compromises to find your "pain points." Then look at the writing you did in the "Setting Intentions" exercise (see page 94). For each pain point, answer this question: What might get me closer to my intentions? Write down everything you can think of, even if it seems impossible.

_____

_____

_____

_____

_____

_____

_____

_____

_____

_____

_____

_____

I WANT TO EXPERIENCE . . .

Meaning often comes from experiences. List some experiences you wish to have.

Five things I want to experience in the next year:

1. _____
2. _____
3. _____
4. _____
5. _____

Five things I want to experience over the next five years:

1. _____
2. _____
3. _____
4. _____
5. _____

I am a role model for living joyfully.
I embrace opportunities to have
fun while sharing my wisdom
and experience with others.

YOUR VISION STATEMENT

Whether you are creating a future that nurtures others or just yourself, having a vision will help you stay on track, persist when you feel tired or discouraged, and find helpers whose values are aligned with yours.

Read over your journal and use your core values, desires, and intentions to answer the following questions.

What do you know so far about what you want to do?

_____

_____

_____

Why does it feel important?

_____

_____

_____

What will it do for you?

_____

_____

_____

What will it do for others?

_____

_____

_____

Goals and Plans

A goal is a finish line. It tells you when you've gotten somewhere. For instance, imagine you made a living teaching kids to dance, but after some injuries, you now see yourself teaching dance to adults with chronic pain. You also need to supplement your retirement income. In this case, your goal might be: "Make enough money to sustain myself teaching dance that eases chronic pain for adults."

Choose one of your intentions, and write it as a goal in the space below.

_____

_____

_____

_____

_____

_____

_____

_____

_____

_____

_____

_____

A plan is a series of steps that leads to the goal. For example:

1. Find out what certifications I need.

2. Take courses on movement for people with chronic pain.

3. Research venues where I can teach.

4. See what jobs are available.

5. Write a proposal to create a job if this doesn't exist yet.

6. Learn about writing grants and marketing if I need to do this independently.

Write your preliminary plan in the space below. Your plan will evolve as you learn more. For now, include anything you know you will need to learn or do to make your goal a reality.

1. _____

2. _____

3. _____

4. _____

5. _____

6. _____

A NO-FAILURE MINDSET

Imagine the concept of failure did not exist. All processes lead to success when your mindset is discovering what works. Every attempt teaches you something useful. Write about pursuing your goals with a no-failure mindset. What would you feel empowered to do?

_____

_____

_____

_____

_____

_____

_____

_____

_____

_____

_____

_____

_____

_____

_____

My second act is perfectly aligned with my values, needs, and vision. Each day feels better than the last as I pursue my dreams.

A FINAL WORD

You did it! You completed your journal of self-discovery. Woo-hoo! This work is just a start, a tool to help you identify your next steps. Taking those steps is your next task. Try to find the sweet spot where you are making progress but not pushing so hard that you feel overwhelmed. Just as you gave this journal 10 minutes a day, give a set time to putting your plans in motion. You can always do more. It's the daily effort that makes things happen.

If you want additional inspiration or ideas, turn to the Resources on the next page. There you'll find books, podcasts, apps, and websites to explore. Reach out for support. Tell people your dreams. Stay open to opportunities and help from unexpected sources. As you learn and grow, be sure to update your goals and your plans. If you're like me, you will have a few favorite exercises that you come back to annually, as your vision evolves. It's also fun to read your journal at the 5- and 10-year marks to see how far you've come. You may discover that you have built a life even better than you imagined.

Once you begin creating a life that feels joyful, motivated by love for yourself and others, a kind of momentum takes hold. It becomes difficult to settle for anything less than joy. You become adept at noticing when things feel off, setting boundaries to get back on track, and pointing yourself toward experiences that fill you up.

I am excited for you. The world needs people who feel fulfilled. I am glad you are becoming one of them.

RESOURCES

Journaling can evoke big feelings and memories that might be hard to deal with alone. If you need support, you can find qualified therapists at:

Psychology Today: PsychologyToday.com—This is a general directory where most therapists are listed.

Therapy Den: TherapyDen.com—This directory is focused on inclusivity and can help you identify therapists who welcome differences of all kinds.

BOOKS

A Long Bright Future by Laura L. Carstensen, PhD—Many of us will live well past eighty. Carstensen provides encouragement and support for creating a second half that is sustainable for decades—physically, financially, and socially.

Choosing Gentleness by Robyn L. Posin, PhD—The second half of life is the perfect time to learn how to tend to ourselves with compassion. Posin's little book on self-care encourages developing a warm and kind relationship with yourself.

WEBSITES

"Kickstart Your Creativity" playlist, TED.com: TED.com/playlists/170/kickstart_your_creativity—If you're feeling stuck and need ideas or inspiration, these TED Talks can help you think outside the box.

VolunteerMatch: VolunteerMatch.org—Explore volunteer opportunities where you can make a difference, make new connections, and discover more of what you love to do.

Good Life Project—Find inspiration and comfort listening to experts in every field talking about happiness, kindness, purpose, and more.

Death, Sex and Money—This podcast ventures into deeper, sometimes darker, questions. If you're looking for opportunities to make a difference, you may find ideas here.

Toobee—This tool sends your affirmations to your mobile on a regular schedule and also has a selection of affirmations if you'd rather not use your own. To make this process work, be sure to stop and take in the affirmation, really feel it, before dismissing the notification.

Acknowledgments

Huge thanks to Rockridge Press for its support in making this journal possible. Deep love and appreciation to all my teachers and everyone who has helped me learn and teach others how to heal, grow, and love themselves unconditionally. To Barbie, Loyd, and all my friends who are my chosen family, and especially to Robyn, whose love is always a soft place to land, I love you to the moon and back.

About the Author

 **Julie A. Levin** is a licensed therapist specializing in self-compassion and self-esteem. Deeply familiar with midlife transitions, Julie opened her psychotherapy practice at the age of forty. After turning fifty, Julie published her first book of poetry, *Walking on Water*. In midlife, Julie has hunted truffles in Italy and become a gourmet vegan cook. She is currently working on her Italian, learning how to play the ukulele, doing yoga, and taking lots of naps.